BILL & KRI
SOUL SHEP

JOURNEY
of the
SOUL

LEADER
GUIDE

ABOUT THE AUTHORS

Bill Gaultiere, PhD is the author of a number of books and resources for soul care. He and his wife Kristi are the founders of Soul Shepherding. Every week they equip thousands of pastors and influencers to thrive with Jesus in life and leadership. They lead their Institute in Spiritual Formation and Soul Care Ministry which includes an optional certificate in Spiritual Direction. They've been speaking at churches and other groups since 1987. For weekly inspiration you can subscribe to their Soul Talks podcast and Soul Shepherding blog.

Bill is a psychologist (PhD; PSY12036in CA), ordained pastor, spiritual director, author, and speaker. As a pastor, he's served in a mega-church and church plant. He's also trained over 1,000 lay counselors and taught courses in Christian psychology and spirituality at the graduate school level. He was personally mentored by Ray Ortlund Sr. and Dallas Willard.

Kristi is a psychotherapist (PsyD; LPC4 and MFT29887 in CA), and spiritual director. As a pastor's wife, mother, and ministry professional, she offers empathy and wisdom from her experience personally and as a therapist who has spent many thousands of hours caring for people. She was personally mentored by Jane Willard and Jan Stoop.

For fun Bill and Kristi enjoy family time, playing with their grandchildren, movies, and taking walks at the ocean.

©2021 Soul Shepherding, Inc.
4000 Barranca Parkway, Suite 250, Irvine, CA 92604
SoulShepherding.org

All Scripture quotations, unless otherwise indicated, are taken from the Holy Bible, New International Version®, NIV®. Copyright ©1973, 1978, 1984, 2011 by Biblica, Inc.™ Used by permission of Zondervan. All rights reserved worldwide. www.zondervan.com The "NIV" and "New International Version" are trademarks registered in the United States Patent and Trademark Office by Biblica, Inc.™

Other Scripture quotations include The New Living Translation (NLT), The Message (MSG), and The Passion Translation (TPT).

GROUP SCHEDULE

WEEK	TOPIC	PAGE

LEADER TOOLS	Leading With Jesus How to Use This Guide Four A's of Empathy Tips to Help Difficult People Group Guidelines	7
1	**JOURNEY OF THE SOUL*** JOTS Chapters 1 & 2	23
2	**DISCIPLESHIP TO JESUS*** JOTS Chapters 3 & 4 (C & H Stages)	33
3	**SERVING GOD** JOTS Chapter 5 (R Stage)	43
4	**THROUGH THE WALL** JOTS Chapter 6	51
5	**YOUR INNER JOURNEY** JOTS Chapter 7 (I Stage)	59
6	**SPACIOUS PLACES*** JOTS Chapters 8 & 9 (S & T Stages)	67
BONUS	**MAKING A JOURNEY MAP** JOTS Chapter 10 Suggestions for Solitude with Jesus	77
HELPFUL TABLES	Stages in Jesus' Life Stages in Psalm 23 Stages & Spiritual Disciplines Stages & Silent Prayer	89

You may want to spend two weeks on these meetings

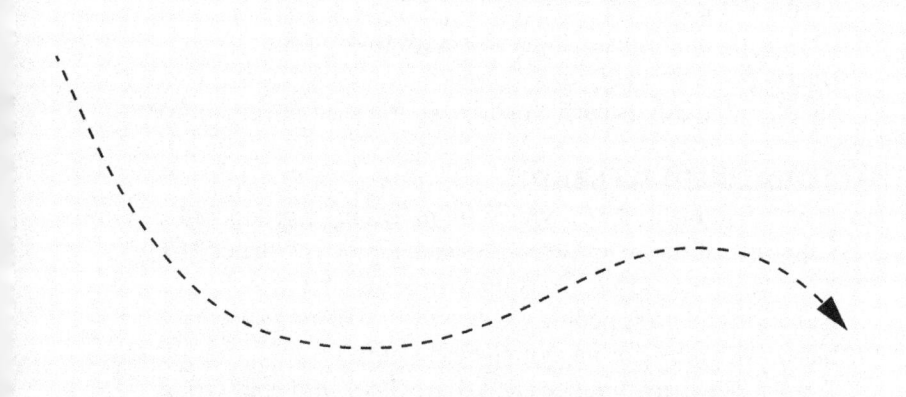

LEADING WITH JESUS

The key to leading your *Journey of the Soul* (*JOTS*) group is leading with Jesus. The purpose of your group is following the Lord Jesus on an adventure of emotional and spiritual growth. In the weeks to come as you read, pray, and lead your group, you and your friends will make wonderful discoveries about authentic discipleship to Jesus that fosters lasting emotional and spiritual growth. The *JOTS* material will guide you and your group along a path through the CHRIST stages of faith and The Wall in the middle that comprise the structure of the book.

This Leader Guide lays out a model for a 6-week small group. We've included extra material for each group gathering so that you have options to choose which content, questions, and activities are most important for your community. As you prepare for leading your meetings, be prayerful about what material is best suited for your group. Also you may want to talk to your group about meeting for more than six weeks. For instance you could spend one week on each of the CHRIST stages, which would make your group eight weeks long.

Specifically, you and your group will gain new insights and practical tools for:
- Keeping Jesus at the center of your heart and life
- Caring for your emotions that are essential to your faith
- Engaging in soul talks

- Choosing the most helpful Scriptures and spiritual disciplines for each CHRIST stage
- Getting through spiritual dryness and stuck places
- Hearing God's voice
- Shepherding others with empathy, gentle wisdom, and prayer

AM I QUALIFIED TO LEAD?

It's easy to feel intimidated when you're leading a group, but you don't need to be a pastor or even a veteran leader. Mostly you need to:
- Be growing in your relationship with Jesus Christ.
- Welcome and bless people.
- Listen with empathy and guide discussion.
- Try new soul care practices and share them with your group.
- Invest a few hours each week to read, pray, prepare, and lead your group.

You'll find that you grow in confidence as a group leader simply by *acting with the Spirit of Jesus.*

SOUL SHEPHERDING LEADERSHIP

Soul Shepherding leadership is following Jesus as we love others into following Jesus with us. It's led and empowered by the Holy Spirit. It's humble, unhurried, compassionate, confident, and adventurous. It's enjoying God's presence in the moment and ministering this to others. Obviously, this kind of spiritual leadership is quite different from worldly leadership that is ego-driven to get power over people and make things happen for selfish reasons.

Practicing these three skills will help you to lead your *JOTS* group as a soul shepherd:

1. LEADING WITH JESUS

The most important way to lead your group is to keep asking Jesus to lead. You're an apprentice to the Master Jesus Christ. Each meeting pray for him to lead and trust him to use the book, group process, and you. Your role is not to teach or push an agenda. Let the material teach and the format guide the process. You're serving as a shepherd who cares for and gently guides people under Jesus the Good Shepherd. At the same time leading with Jesus is not passive. You're joining in his work to love God and people well. Your group needs you as the human leader helping them to listen to and learn from the Lord Jesus.

2 GIVING EMPATHY

Empathy is listening to and caring for people's feelings, desires, and needs. It's especially powerful when they sense that you're genuinely glad to be with them and understand them. Your empathy helps them to trust Jesus and experience God's presence. If you're able some weeks to go the extra mile and check in with group members it will add to them feeling cared for. A simple text or Instagram message saying you're praying for someone is a huge blessing (see "Four A's of Empathy" below).

3 PRACTICING QUIET PRAYER

The soul care practices in *Journey of the Soul* facilitate personal experiences in quietly meditating on Scripture. These spiritual disciplines facilitate deepening discipleship to Jesus, self-awareness, and group bonding. However, some people in your group may be inexperienced or uncomfortable with quiet prayer. So this leader guide directs you to use these exercises in private to intercede for your group and then in the meetings to take little steps with very short periods of silence. Some groups will be comfortable with more silent reflection and others will need to do the practices on their own and process in the group. To lead others well in quiet prayer you need to practice it on your own so that in group you're relaxed as you enjoy God's presence and can minister this to your community.

SUPPORTING RESOURCES

To foster spiritual growth for you and your group and to support your leadership Bill and Kristi have created some additional *JOTS* resources which you can find on journeyofthesoul.org:

- Free sermon outlines to go with each small group meeting
- Short videos introducing the *JOTS* content for each meeting
- Free Soul Shepherding playlists of worship songs for each of the CHRIST stages and The Wall (e.g., "C Stage: Journey of the Soul")
- Deck of Soul Talk cards to make it fun to learn the CHRIST stages and deepen your relationship with God and your friends!

SHARING THE JOURNEY

Thank you for partnering with Soul Shepherding by discipling people to love and serve Jesus! You'll be encouraged to see how much more you learn and grow by serving in this role. It'd be awesome if you'd share your experience in your circle of influence. Here are some ways you can do that:

- Write a book review on Amazon for *Journey of the Soul*.
- Take a picture with your small group and share it on your social media feeds, tagging your friends, and adding the hashtag #JOTSbook.
- Share Soul Shepherding's podcasts, blog, playlists, and social media posts in your networks.

HOW TO USE THIS GUIDE

This Leader Guide takes you deeper into the material in *Journey of the Soul: A Practical Guide to Emotional and Spiritual Growth*. It shows you step-by-step how to assist Jesus in leading your group meetings and shepherding the people in your group. The format of each week includes these helpful sections:
- Overview
- To Do List before the meeting
- Empathy guidance
- Prayer points
- JOTS chapter summaries
- Detailed outline for your group time
- Tips for leading well

The next four pages offer a quick visual tour of the features that will help you lead your group.

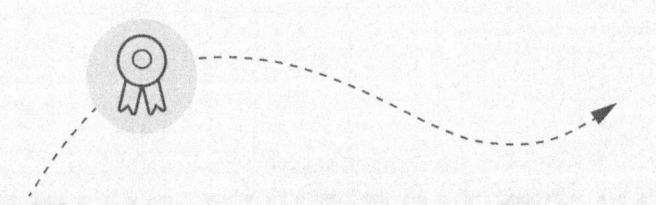

Week 3
SERVING GOD

LEADER PREP
Overview

To follow Jesus means we're joining h[...]
people. It honors God and draws peopl[...]
people or use our spiritual gifts to help [...]
every stage of faith, but especially in "Res[...]
when we have new knowledge, oppor[...]
others. Sharing with others from what t[...]

In your *JOTS* group there may be a few p[...]
churches have lots of people in this stag[...]
we stretch ourselves to serve others in [...]
and this helps us to experience belonging and significance.

> The Leader Prep includes several pages that walk you through the steps to prepare for each meeting, including a brief summary of the corresponding chapter(s) from *Journey of the Soul* (*JOTS*).

LEADER TOOLS: HOW TO USE THIS GUIDE

WEEK 3: SERVI

GROUP TIME

WELCOME (5 MINUTES)
- Greet everyone with a smile and
  coming.
- Share your excitement to learn together about serving God and blessing people in the stage of Responsibilities in Ministry (or R Stage).
- Reinforce group guidelines like keeping shares brief, listening without giving advice, and confidentiality (*Leader Guide*, pp. 21-22).
- Ask someone who is willing to open in prayer.

FUN ACTIVITY (5 MINUTES)

> **TIP**
> Your joyful love for Jesus will help the group to bond as his servants.

- Invite everyone to join you and c
  and serving God.
- Lead them in skipping like a child
  "I'm the disciple Jesus loves! I'm
  disciple Jesus loves!"

SCRIPTURE READING (5 MINUTES)
- Invite group members to read out
  Stage (*JOTS*, p. 109).

INTRODUCE R STAGE (15 MINUTES)

> **TIP**
> Affirm the great value of people's talents and desires for serving God.

- Play one of the worship songs from the Soul Shepherding playlist "R Stage: Journey of the Soul" or encourage people to listen on their own (see journeyofthesoul.org).
- Share with your group this week's *JOTS* video on "Serving God" (see journeyofthesoul.org).

47

> You can adjust these times. You can also choose what group material to cover and what to leave out. Do what's best for your group and be sure to end your group on time.

> At times it will be helpful to ask your group to turn to the page(s) in *JOTS* so they can see the diagram, table, story, or quote you're referencing.

JOURNAL OF THE SOUL: **LEADER GUIDE**

- Read the key Scripture for *JOTS* chapter five (see above) and comment briefly on why you like it.
- Read two or three of your favorite quotes (see above) and comment briefly on why you like them.
- Ask the group, "What stood out to you in this chapter with Jesus? Or maybe you have a question."

> **TIP**
> Offer empathy for any stress, frustration, or discouragement people feel in this stage.

SOUL TALK (30 MINUTES)

> **TIP**
> You may not have time for all the soul talk questions below. Choose the ones you believe are most helpful for your group.

> These Soul Talk questions steer people away from giving opinions or advice and invite them to share their personal experiences related to their discipleship to Jesus.

1. *Optional*: What were your peak and valley experiences? How did you sense God's presence in these situations?

2. Which of the false identities or lies do you struggle with? (I am what I do, I am what I have, I am what others say about me.)

> **TIP**
> Cultivate and affirm people's trust in Jesus to guide and empower their leadership or service.

> These practical tips help you guide group sharing and process. These are spiritual director skills made simple.

3. How does it feel to identify yourself as the disciple Jesus loves? What helps you to live that way?

4. Which joy gift(s) do you most enjoy using to serve others? How does this feel for you?

48

LEADER TOOLS: **HOW TO USE THIS GUIDE**

WEEK 3: **SERVING GOD**

> **TIP**
> Affirm the "little" acts of care, kindness, or prayer that people offer as the greatest exar

5. Which of "Elijah's disciplines" of se life now? (e.g., sleep, healthy food soul talk, being quiet and still, del 105-107).

> These times of praying Scripture foster personal experiences with God for you and your group.

SOUL CARE PRACTICE (15 MINUTES)
- Invite anyone who wants to do so to share briefly about their experience last week with practicing what they're learning in group.
- Comment briefly on the value of quietly meditating on Scripture for growing in discipleship to Jesus.
- Prayerfully read the guided meditation on "Christ goes ahead of you," leaving quiet pauses after each part (*JOTS*, pp. 111-112).
- After the meditation invite people to share briefly on their thoughts or feelings during the experience.

SET UP NEXT MEETING (2 MINUTES
Ask your group participants to:
- Read *Journey of the Soul* chapter six 115).
- Experiment with the soul care pract at the end of chapter six (*JOTS*, p.
- Listen to the worship songs on th Wall: Journey of the Soul" (see jour

> Prayer is the most important aspect of your group! This Leader Guide helps you pray before group, at the start, and at the end.

CLOSING PRAYER (1 MINUTE)
- Ask someone who is willing to close the group with a short prayer.
- Or if time allows take prayer requests and ask group members to pray for each other.

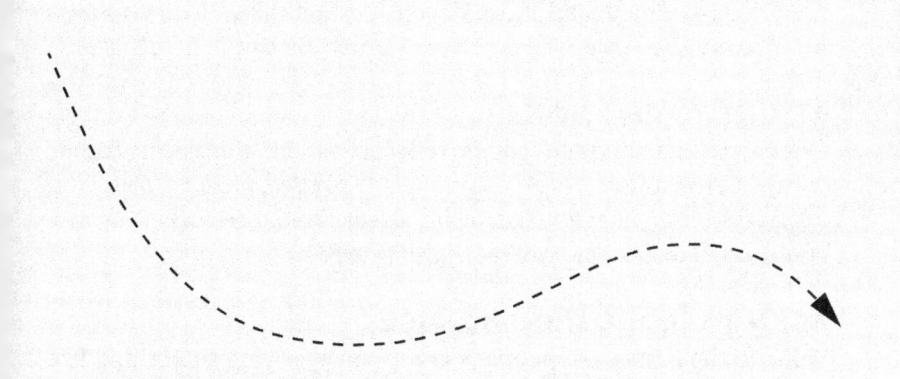

FOUR A'S OF EMPATHY

Empathy is vastly underrated and in short supply in our world. When you offer empathy to your group members it will be a huge blessing to them.

What is emapthy? It's putting yourself in someone else's skin to feel what it's like to be that person. It's listening with an open heart, being curious and asking questions, resisting advice or cheerleading, being nonjudgmental, offering warmth and acceptance, reflecting back the emotions you're sensing, summarizing the key points you're hearing, and offering silent little prayers as you listen.

Empathy is oxygen for our souls. It's essential for spiritual growth. It promotes self-awareness, bonding in relationships, trusting God, hearing God's voice, insights on Scripture and discipleship, and love for God and other people. It's the source of effective compassion, kindness, and love. It's also a main source of wisdom and effective leadership. Empathy helps us to feel God's presence and receive the grace we need.

Perfect empathy is Jesus, the holy Son of God, setting aside the privileges of deity and heaven and taking on human flesh to live in our world, experience our life and suffering, and even take on our sin. Perfect empathy is Jesus choosing to sacrifice his life for us on the cross so that we could be forgiven, reconciled to God, and receive new life.

1. **ASK TO TALK**
   Be curious to understand and ask open questions like, *"What would you like to share? How are you feeling? What more do you have to say about this?"*

2. **ATTUNE TO EMOTIONS**
   Offer active listening and mirror (reflect back) emotions using feeling words. For instance, *"It seems you feel __[stressed, anxious, frustrated, angry, discouraged, guilty, sad, alone, disappointed, rejected]__."* Or you could say, *"I understand you're struggling with _____."*

3. **ACKNOWLEDGE SIGNIFICANCE**
   Validate the bigness of people's emotions by saying something like, *"Feeling _____ is a huge issue for you."* Or *"This situation is very painful for you."*

4. **AFFIRM STRENGTHS**
   Offer encouraging words and appreciate good qualities. This is most effective when offered after empathizing with emotional struggles. Examples include, *"You're doing valuable inner work."* Or *"I admire your courage to be honest."*

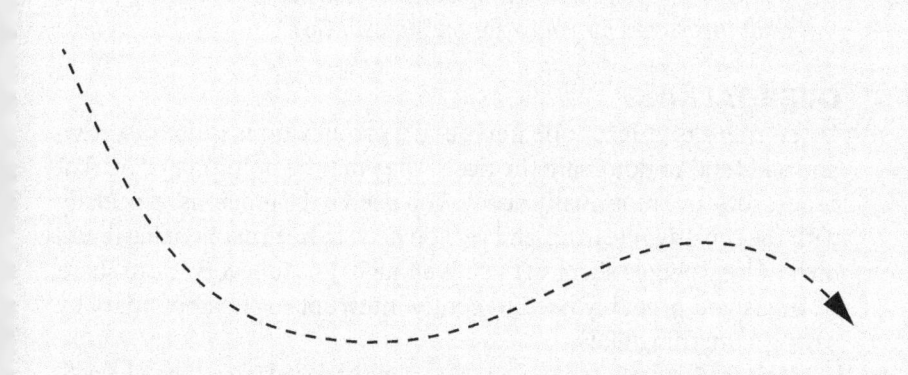

TIPS TO HELP DIFFICULT PEOPLE

In your *JOTS* group there are people with different backgrounds, personalities, and CHRIST stages and their differing desires or styles may cause friction. Some people will need coaching to understand and support the group process. Here are some common difficulties in groups with thoughts on how to respond:

1. **LATE FOR GROUP**
   When people are late it's tempting to start the group late. It's important for you as the leader to hold to the agreed on times to start and end each group. (You may decide it's best to allow five to ten minutes for people to connect and settle before beginning the group time.) This shows respect for everyone and encourages them to value the time. It also motivates those who were late to be on time for the next meeting.

2. **HEAD TYPES**
   Analytical people think deeply about a subject before they share. When they do share they tend to go into a heady or teaching mode rather than sharing their personal experience and learning. If they go on too long you may need to interrupt them and say something like:
   - *" _[Name]_ , You've got some great ideas about this. What is your personal experience?"*

- *"It sounds like you could teach on this subject, but for this group tell us what this means for your relationship with God."*

3. **OVER-TALKING**
   Often there is at least one person in a group who is quite talkative and will tend to dominate the time. They may be opinionated, verbal processors, or emotionally needy. You need to be gracious, especially with the sensitive-hearted, and yet you need to be firm in setting limits on how long people share so there is enough time for everyone to share. At times you probably need to gently interrupt to set a boundary by saying something like:
   - *"I understand you feel _____. I wish we had more time, but right now we need to hear from others."*
   - *" _[Name]_ , let's give someone else a chance to share now."*
   - *"I'm sorry to interrupt, but we're running out of time and we need to get into our meditation."*

4. **ADVICE-GIVING, DEBATING, AND JUDGING**
   The group is designed for people to briefly share their personal experiences, what they're learning, or prayer requests. Giving advice, strong opinions, or making judgements are hurtful to people and disrupts the group process. You need to set strong and loving boundaries to protect individuals and the community. You may need to say something like:
   - *" _[Name]_ , I hear you have some strong ideas. I'd like for you to talk with me about this later."*
   - *" _[Name]_ , Those are interesting thoughts. I'd like to hear more about that in another setting, but in our group we need to protect space for each person to share their personal experience and receive empathetic listening and prayer."*

5. **SHYNESS**
   Some people in your group may be shy. On one hand they need your warmth and friendliness, but on the other they need space to decline to share and not be pressured. If a group member has been quiet for awhile it's good to check in and say something like:
   - *" _[Name]_ , what would you like to share about this? We'd love to hear from you, but if you want to pass it's fine."*

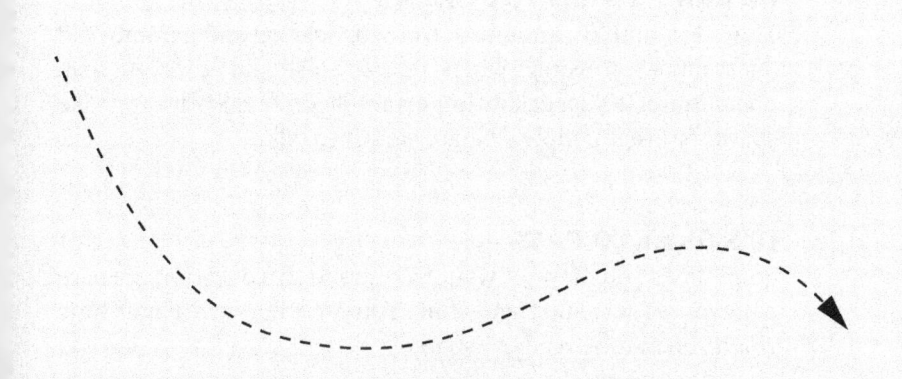

GROUP GUIDELINES

As a group leader it's important for you to protect the purposes of the group and the emotional safety and well-being of each member. To help you do that it's good to read these guidelines out loud in your group the first couple of meetings. You can lead into this by saying, "We have a few guidelines that will help our group be a great experience of growing discipleship to Jesus in which we love one another well."

1. **COME PREPARED**
   To receive all God has for you in this group read the chapter(s) and soul care practice(s) that correspond with each meeting.

2. **KEEP CONFIDENTIALITY**
   When people share personal information it needs to be kept secret and not shared with other people.

3. **SHARE PERSONALLY**
   When you share in group please do not give your opinions, teach your insights, or talk about other people. Instead use "I" statements in which you invite others to understand you personal experience, emotions, or needs.

4. BE BRIEF WHEN YOU SHARE
There is a limited amount of time for sharing and a number of questions so on average when you share it should be for less than one minute. It's especially important if you're talkative to make space for other people who are slower to talk.

5. IT'S OKAY TO PASS
Sometimes you may not want to respond to a question or share a prayer request and that is fine. You can wait until a later time when you may be ready to share.

6. LISTEN WITH EMPATHY - DON'T GIVE ADVICE
When people share with the group don't give your insights or try to fix their problem. Instead open your heart to listen to their experience, feel their emotions, and quietly pray for them. Trust the Spirit of Jesus to use the group material to lead people into truth.

7. PRACTICE SILENCE
When we pray Scripture there will be time for quiet reflection. You may feel distracted or antsy. Repeating the Bible phrase in your mind, imagining Jesus, or focusing on your breathing can help you to be emotionally present. (These ideas can also help you quietly listen to other people.)

8. ARRIVE ON TIME
Plan to arrive five minutes early to help you be on time. This will also help you to be unhurried and to love others well. But if you are late the group will welcome you and give you grace.

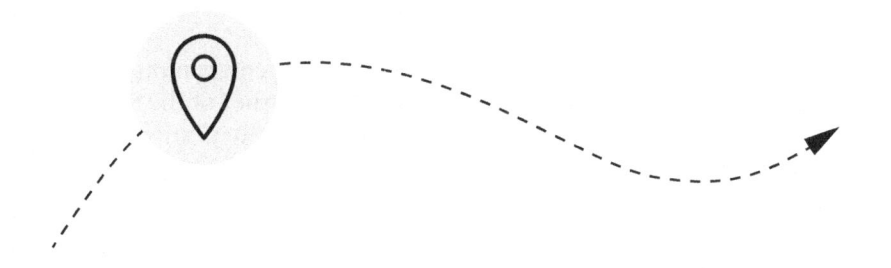

Week 1
JOURNEY OF THE SOUL

LEADER PREP
Overview

Many people get lost, stalled, or sidetracked in their journey with Jesus but don't know how to proceed because they don't understand where they are. The CHRIST stages of faith offer you a map of your soul that says, "You are here!" When you know which developmental phase you're currently experiencing or whether you're at The Wall then you can see your path ahead for growing in emotional and spiritual health.

The people in your group are likely in different stages of the journey, but most church attenders are in one of the first three stages. As a group leader you can make a big difference by helping people to understand the CHRIST stages and identify which stage(s) they are currently experiencing. As you support and gently guide your group through the material in the book *Journey of the Soul (JOTS)* they will be greatly encouraged in their discipleship to Jesus and next steps of growth.

> **TO DO LIST**
>
> - Read JOTS chapters 1 and 2 and this leader guide.
> - Visit journeyofthesoul.org for resources to lead your group each week.
> - Choose a song to share in group from the Soul Shepherding playlist "C Stage: Journey of the Soul."
> - Watch the companion video "Journey of the Soul" and arrange to share it in group.
> - Pray for your group (see below).

Empathy

As a group leader the most important thing you can do to help people on their journey with Jesus is to be empathetic. When they arrive they'll be checking out your group. By welcoming each person with joy and showing genuine interest in their life then they will want to learn and grow with you. By being a fellow student of Jesus' — learning the JOTS material and doing the soul care practices — this will guide your prayers for them and it will help you find words to describe their struggles and hopes so they can better understand where they are in the journey and explore their next steps.

> **PRAYER POINTS**
>
> - Ask Jesus to shepherd group members in the stages of faith so they grow in emotional and spiritual health.
> - Pray for group members to experience God's grace.
> - Pray for them to be encouraged by the Psalm 23 meditation and Paul's story of grace.

SHEPHERDING YOUR SOUL
Journey of the Soul Chapter 1 Summary

> **THEME**
> **TO THRIVE IN YOUR LIFE WITH JESUS YOU NEED SOUL CARE AND GUIDANCE.**

KEY SCRIPTURE
"Jesus says, 'I am the good shepherd; I know my sheep and my sheep know me.'" *John 10:14*

CHRIST STAGES (SEE DESCRIPTIONS ON *JOTS*, PP. 27-28)
- **C**onfidence in Christ
- **H**elp in Discipleship
- **R**esponsibilities in Ministry
- The Wall (transition)
- **I**nner Journey
- **S**pirit-Led Ministry
- **T**ransforming Union

KEY QUOTES
- "Healthy faith engages our soul on a path of following Christ Jesus through six stages of emotional and spiritual development" (*JOTS*, p. 25).
- "Your soul [or whole person], well cared for by God, invigorates and integrates all the functions of your being — emotions, thoughts, intentions, body, and relationships — into a *flow of joyful, abundant, powerful, divine, and eternal life expressed in your unique personality*" (*JOTS*, pp. 25-26).
- "At times we all need... a soul map with personalized guidance for [our] spiritual pilgrimage on the Way of Jesus" (*JOTS*, pp. 26-27).
- "Your progression through the CHRIST stages (or phases) of faith is not linear but circular.... because emotional and spiritual growth in God's grace is an up-and-down journey in which we go back and forth between developmental phases" (*JOTS*, p. 28).
- "Spiritual disciplines are bodily activities you can practice to develop habits to rely on Jesus, care for your soul, and love God and people well. Certain disciplines work best at each stage but often you can benefit from the ones in previous stages" (*JOTS*, p. 30).

- "Henri Nouwen put it well: 'There is no journey to God outside of the journey that Jesus made'" (*JOTS*, p. 31).

KEY TERMS (SEE DESCRIPTIONS ON *JOTS*, P. 30)	
Soul	Whole person
CHRIST Stages	Each stage of faith builds on the next
Home Stage	Your primary stage
Roadblocks	Trials that tempt us to turn back to previous stage
First Half and Second Half	Three stages on either side of The Wall
Grace	God's favor and power
Faith	Responding to God's grace with trust
Spiritual Disciplines	Bodily activities to learn to love; different ones work best at different stages

GRACE FOR YOUR JOURNEY
Journey of the Soul Chapter 2 Summary

> **THEME**
> **YOU GROW BY RELYING ON GOD'S FAVOR AND POWER IN THE UPS AND DOWNS OF LIFE.**

KEY SCRIPTURE
"God saved you by his grace when you believed. And you can't take credit for this; it is a gift from God. Salvation is not a reward for the good things we have done, so none of us can boast about it. For we are God's masterpiece. He has created us anew in Christ Jesus, so we can do the good things he planned for us long ago." *Ephesians 2:8-10 NLT*

KEY QUOTES
- "[In] the Cycle of Works . . . the pressure is on for achievement in our work, family, church, physical appearance, social media, or whatever we're into" (*JOTS*, p. 41).
- "When we think of grace only as either forgiveness or a transaction that happened at the cross, then we miss out on the joy of a friendly and empowering relationship with Jesus" (*JOTS*, p. 43).
- "[Brennan Manning] keeps reminding me, 'God loves you as you are and not as you should be!' He assures me that the Abba of Jesus is very fond of me" (*JOTS*, p. 43).
- "As Dallas Willard liked to say, 'Grace is not opposed to effort, it is opposed to earning'" (*JOTS*, p. 43).
- "*Consolation* refers to times in which we feel the warmth of God's presence or the sense that we're blessed and encouraged by our Lord" (*JOTS*, p. 46).
- "In times of *desolation*, blessed feelings evaporate and God seems far away" (*JOTS*, p. 47).
- "Our opportunity [in desolation] is to keep trusting that God truly loves us and is growing us in the CHRIST stages of faith even when we don't see it or feel it" (*JOTS*, p. 47).
- "At each stage you'll face a roadblock in the form of a personal struggle or other trials. You'll also find a wonderful opportunity for a new experience of God's abundant grace that can help you to grow in your identity in Christ" (*JOTS*, p. 50).

CHRIST STAGES SUMMARY

Stage	Ages	Roadblock	Grace
C	3 to adult	Soul splits	Sticky love
H	7 to adult	Misinterpreting Scripture	God's Word in community
R	13 to adult	False identity	Joy gifts for serving God
Wall	18+ (esp midlife)	Distrusting God	God's empathy
I	Usually 30+ (if ever)	Denial of emotions	Experiencing God's love
S	Usually 40+ (if ever)	Dark Night of the Soul	Surprise blessings
T	Usually 60+ (if ever)	Diminishing Jesus Christ	Practicing God's presence

GROUP TIME

WELCOME (5 MINUTES)
- Greet everyone with a smile and enthusiasm. Thank them for joining you in this journey of the soul.

> **TIP**
> It helps your group feel God's love when you smile and say something like, "I'm glad to see you!"

- Share your excitement to learn together about growing in grace from the first two chapters in *Journey of the Soul*.
- Read out loud the group guidelines (*Leader Guide*, pp. 21-22).
- Ask someone who is willing to open in prayer.

SCRIPTURE READING (5 MINUTES)
- Invite group members to read out loud a favorite Scripture insight on Jesus' modeling of the CHRIST stages in chapter one (*JOTS*, pp. 31-33).
- Invite group members to read out loud a favorite Scripture insight on God's grace in chapter two (*JOTS*, p. 45).

INTRODUCE GRACE FOR THE JOURNEY (15 MINUTES)
- Play one of the worship songs from the Soul Shepherding playlist "C Stage: Journey of the Soul" or encourage people to listen on their own (see journeyofthesoul.org).

> **TIP**
> Tell your group how it's blessed you to listen to the songs in the *Journey of the Soul* playlists.

- Share with your group the first video on "Journey of the Soul" (see journeyofthesoul.org).
- Read the key Scriptures for *JOTS* chapters one and two (see above) and comment briefly on why you like them.
- Briefly discuss the Cycle of Works and Cycle of Grace (*JOTS*, pp. 40-41).
- Ask the group, "What stood out to you about Jesus' and Paul's journeys through the CHRIST stages?" (*JOTS*, pp. 31-33 and 45).

> **TIP**
> Guard the group guidelines so that people who share receive listening and empathy — not advice or cheerleading.

SOUL TALK (35 MINUTES)

> **TIP**
> You may not have time for all the soul talk questions below. Choose the ones you believe are most helpful for your group.

1. What were your peak and pit this past week? How did you sense God's presence in these situations?

> **TIP**
> When someone shares a personal experience briefly reflect back their emotions by saying something like, "It seems you feel _____."

2. What are your thoughts about life being a journey with Jesus that goes through stages of emotional and spiritual growth?

3. What is something you appreciated about Jesus' own journey through the CHRIST stages?

4. What helps you move out of the Cycle of Works and into the Cycle of Grace?

5. In the past when you experienced spiritual desolation what helped you receive grace from God?

6. What is something from Paul's story of grace that is helpful for you?

SOUL CARE PRACTICE (15 MINUTES)

> **TIP**
> Lead the soul care practice with a gentle voice and leave some quiet spaces for private reflection and prayer.

- Comment briefly on the value of praying Scripture for experiencing God's grace.
- Share with your group the Psalm 23 Meditation by Kristi Gaultiere (*JOTS*, pp. 35-38 or listen to the Soul Talks podcast E112, "Selah: Psalm 23"). Or read Psalm 23 out loud slowly and leave quiet pauses between phrases.
- After the meditation invite people to share briefly on their thoughts or feelings during the experience.

SET UP NEXT MEETING (5 MINUTES)
Ask your group members to:
- Read *Journey of the Soul* chapter three on "Confidence in Christ" (*JOTS*, p. 59) and chapter four on "Help in Discipleship" (*JOTS*, p. 75).
- Experiment with the soul care practice on "Delighting in the Lord" at the end of chapter three (*JOTS*, p. 73) or "Jesus' Pocket Lighter" at the end of chapter four (*JOTS*, p. 91).
- Listen to the worship songs on the Soul Shepherding playlists, "C Stage: Journey of the Soul" and "H Stage: Journey of the Soul" (see journeyofthesoul.org).

CLOSING PRAYER (1 MINUTE)
- Ask someone who is willing to close the group with a short prayer.

> **TIP**
> Snap a group picture and post it on your social media. Be sure to tag your group members and use #JOTSbook.

Week 2
DISCIPLESHIP TO JESUS

LEADER PREP
Overview

We're learning how to grow in emotional and spiritual health as we follow Jesus Christ. In this session we explore Confidence in Christ (C Stage) and Help in Discipleship (H Stage), the first two CHRIST stages of faith in *Journey of the Soul* (chapters three and four). To follow Jesus is to be his disciple or apprentice. For each of us this means we say, "I want to learn how to live my life as Jesus would live it if he were me." With the help of the Holy Spirit we can learn how to be fully alive and fully loving in our relationships, work, and all we do!

Some of the people in your JOTS group are probably in the C and H Stages. As new Christ-followers or people who are rededicating their lives to Christ they can bring to the community wonder, fresh energy, teachableness, and appreciation. You may have seekers in your group who are approaching the C Stage. Probably you have people with past experience with the C and H Stages. Whatever the mix in your group, everyone needs to strengthen the foundation of their faith. As a leader you can support them to set (or re-set) a wise and healthy course for their journey with Jesus.

TO DO LIST

☐ Read JOTS chapters 3 and 4 and this leader guide.

☐ Watch the companion video "Discipleship to Jesus" and arrange to share it in group.

☐ Choose a song to share in group from the Soul Shepherding playlist "H Stage: Journey of the Soul."

☐ Pray for your group (see below).

Empathy

Group members in the Confidence in Christ and Help in Discipleship Stages will especially struggle with distractions, sin, and guilt. Often they're focused on their personal needs or faith questions and want advice or reassurance, but actually what they need is to learn to trust God with their problems and take personal responsibility for their growth. In leading your group be careful not to be too directive or over-teach. Instead, serve as an empathetic listener and guide.

PRAYER POINTS

☐ Ask Jesus to lead the group so people feel safe to share their faith stories and learn from one another.

☐ Pray for group members to grow in their discipleship to Jesus.

☐ Pray for them to delight in the Lord and learn to pray Scripture with their heart.

CONFIDENCE IN CHRIST (C STAGE)
Journey of the Soul Chapter 3 Summary

> **THEME**
> **FOLLOWING JESUS BEGINS WITH RECEIVING HIS FORGIVENESS AND NEW LIFE.**

KEY SCRIPTURE
"Praise be to the God and Father of our Lord Jesus Christ! In his great mercy he has given us new birth into a living hope through the resurrection of Jesus Christ from the dead." *1 Peter 1:3*

TRAIL MARKERS: C STAGE (SEE FULL TABLE ON *JOTS*, P. 70)

1st CHRIST stage

Age	3 to adult
Cognitive Development	Experiential and imaginative
Roadblock	Soul splits (torn between the world and God's kingdom)
Grace	Sticky love (the grace of Jesus that helps us bond with God)
Spiritual Disciplines	Noticing God in nature, learning from spiritual leaders, reading Bible stories, attending church, praying about personal needs

KEY QUOTES

- "Abraham has chutzpah — he ventures out into the unknown with audacious belief in his loving Lord" (Gen. 15:6, Ja. 2:23; *JOTS*, p. 61).
- "Your story of faith is precious and unique to you. It's a story that needs to be told, nurtured, and developed" (*JOTS*, p. 62).
- "[In the C Stage] we're in a tug-of-war between the kingdoms of light and darkness (Col. 1:13)" (*JOTS*, p. 65).
- "Peter's *heart* (spirit) was determined to be faithful to Jesus, but his *flesh* (natural human ability) was habituated in pride and anger. He had a soul split" (Mark 14:38; *JOTS*, p. 65).
- "Empathy is vastly under appreciated — it's a palpable way that the Holy Spirit ministers to us the sticky love of Christ that restores our soul splits" (*JOTS*, p. 67).
- "The best way for children and adults to cultivate heart-trust in God is by accessing their emotional brain along with their rational brain" (*JOTS*, p. 69).
- "Even when you're emotional or needy or when you've sinned, *Jesus delights to know you and care for you*" (*JOTS*, p. 73).

HELP IN DISCIPLESHIP (H STAGE)
Journey of the Soul Chapter 4 Summary

> **THEME**
> **WE GROW BY BEING IN COMMUNITY WITH CHRIST-FOLLOWERS AND PRACTICING SPIRITUAL DISCIPLINES.**

KEY SCRIPTURE
"Train yourself to be godly. For physical training is of some value, but godliness has value for all things, holding promise for both the present life and the life to come." *1 Timothy 4:7-8*

TRAIL MARKERS: H STAGE (SEE FULL TABLE ON *JOTS*, P. 87)

2nd CHRIST stage	
Age	7 to adult
Cognitive Development	Concrete and linear
Roadblock	Misinterpreting Scripture
Grace	God's word in community (learning from Scripture together)
Spiritual Disciplines	Being discipled, church involvement, daily devotions, praying the Lord's prayer, memorizing Bible verses, small groups

BIBLICAL BLUNDERS (SEE EXPLANATIONS ON *JOTS*, PP. 79-82)
- "Be perfect"
- "Do not feel anxious"
- "Just have faith"
- "Hate yourself"

KEY QUOTES
- "We want to be like Mary Magdalene who in the H Stage kept growing closer to her beloved Teacher and gave him the affectionate nickname 'Rabboni' (John 20:16)" (*JOTS*, p. 78).
- "We need to integrate feeling and thinking in our Bible study and soul care" (*JOTS*, p. 79).
- "In the H Stage we're prone to be strong but stupid, having zeal without knowledge" (*JOTS*, p. 82).
- "Every Christian needs some older Christian they're learning from and some younger Christian they're teaching" (Ray Ortlund Sr; see 2 Tim. 2:2; *JOTS*, p. 84).
- "'Don't try — train' (see 1 Tim. 4:7)... means asking Jesus to coach you in using some key disciplines as means of grace" (*JOTS*, p. 85).
- "Adam's previous habit of lusting needed to be replaced with a new habit of finding sweet sufficiency in Christ (Col. 3:5, 11)" (*JOTS*, p. 85).
- "I want your heart to be stirred [by using Jesus' prayer] 'as a pocket lighter to kindle a flame in the heart'" (Martin Luther, *JOTS*, p. 90).

WEEK 2: DISCIPLESHIP TO JESUS

GROUP TIME

WELCOME (5 MINUTES)
- Greet everyone with a smile and enthusiasm and thank them for coming.

> **TIP**
> Encourage your group by reminding them that following Jesus is the best life!

- Share your excitement to learn together about the first two CHRIST stages of Confidence in Christ (or the C Stage) and Help in Discipleship (or the H Stage).
- Read out loud the group guidelines (*Leader Guide*, pp. 21-22).
- Ask someone who is willing to open in prayer.

SCRIPTURE READING (5 MINUTES)

> **TIP**
> The simple act of reading a Scripture out loud helps people warm up to sharing in the community.

- Invite group members to read out loud a favorite Scripture for the C Stage (*JOTS*, p. 71).
- Invite group members to read out loud a favorite Scripture for the H Stage (*JOTS*, p. 88).

INTRODUCE C & H STAGES (15 MINUTES)
- Play one of the worship songs from the Soul Shepherding playlist "H Stage: Journey of the Soul" or encourage people to listen on their own (see journeyofthesoul.org).
- Share with your group this week's *JOTS* video on "Discipleship to Jesus" (see journeyofthesoul.org).
- Read the key Scriptures for *JOTS* chapters three and four (see above) and comment briefly on why you like them.
- Read two or three of your favorite quotes from *JOTS* chapters three and four (see above) and comment briefly on why you like them.

> **TIP**
> Group comments and questions facilitate learning and community. If needed allow quiet pauses of up to 10 seconds for people to share.

- Ask the group, "What stood out to you about the C and H stages in the journey with Jesus? Or maybe you have a question?"

> **TIP**
> Empathize with people's struggles and affirm their longings for God.

SOUL TALK (35 MINUTES)

> **TIP**
> You may not have time for all the soul talk questions below. Choose the ones you believe are the most helpful for your group.

1. *Optional*: What were your peak and pit this past week? How did you sense God's presence in these situations?

2. Why is it important to begin our faith journey trusting in God as merciful and gracious?

> **TIP**
> Affirm the lovingkindness of God in the face of Jesus.

3. What do you think about the idea that we are torn between the kingdoms of Christ and Satan?

4. What helps you appreciate that God's sticky love is better than anything else in life (Ps. 63:3)?

5. Which of the Biblical blunders have you struggled with?

> **TIP**
> If people make unwise choices, resist the urge to moralize (e.g., "Oh, you shouldn't have...") or reassure (e.g., "Well, God can work it our for good"). Instead ask how they feel about it or what their prayer request is.

6. What is an example of how participating in church has fostered your discipleship to Jesus?

SOUL CARE PRACTICE (15 MINUTES)

> **TIP**
> Lead this soul care space with a gentle voice and leave some quiet spaces for private reflection and prayer.

- Invite anyone who wants to do so to share briefly about their experience last week with practicing what they're learning in group.
- Comment briefly on the value of quietly meditating on Scripture for growing in discipleship to Jesus.
- Slowly read out loud "Jesus' Pocket Lighter" (a paraphrase of the Lord's Prayer), pausing quietly after each line, and leaving about thirty seconds for silent prayer at the end (*JOTS*, p. 91).
- After the meditation invite people to share briefly on their thoughts or feelings during the experience.

SET UP NEXT MEETING (2 MINUTES)

> **TIP**
> Encourage people to experiment on their own with a soul care practice for deeper personal experience and lasting change.

Ask your group participants to:
- Read *JOTS* chapter five on "Responsibilities in Ministry" (*JOTS*, p. 93).
- Experiment with the soul care practice on "Working with Christ" at the end of chapter five (*JOTS*, p. 110).

- Listen to the worship songs on the Soul Shepherding playlist, "R Stage: Journey of the Soul" (see journeyofthesoul.org).

CLOSING PRAYER (1 MINUTE)
- Ask someone who is willing to close the group with a short prayer.
- Or if time allows you can take prayer requests and ask group members to pray briefly for each other.

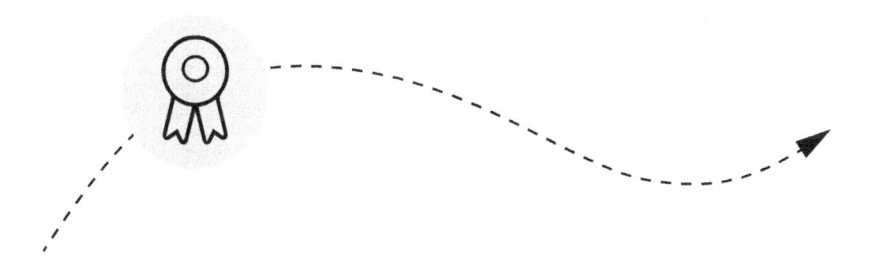

Week 3
SERVING GOD

LEADER PREP
Overview

To follow Jesus means we're joining him to serve God by loving other people. It honors God and draws people to Jesus whenever we're kind to people or use our spiritual gifts to help them. Serving God is important in every stage of faith, but especially in "Responsibilities in Ministry" (R Stage) when we have new knowledge, opportunities, and confidence to bless others. Sharing with others from what the Lord has given us is a great joy.

In your *JOTS* group there may be a few people people in the R Stage, as most churches have lots of people in this stage. That's because it's the stage that we stretch ourselves to serve others in our church, community, and world and this helps us to experience belonging and significance.

TO DO LIST

- [ ] Read *JOTS* chapter 5 and this leader guide.
- [ ] Watch the companion video "Serving God" and arrange to share it in group.
- [ ] Choose a song to share in group from the Soul Shepherding playlist "R Stage: Journey of the Soul."
- [ ] Pray for your group (see below).

Empathy

People who are newer in Responsibilities in Ministry need help to discover and use their spiritual gifts. As they serve God they will get tired and discouraged at times and prone to spiritual dryness or burnout and need your empathy, prayers, and encouragement. Everyone in your group, whatever their CHRIST stage, needs to appreciate God's loving presence, including through other people, in order to be strengthened for the work of loving other people for Jesus' sake.

PRAYER POINTS

- [ ] Ask Jesus to lead the group so people feel encouraged as they explore serving God in the R Stage.

- [ ] Pray for group members to use their spiritual gift(s) to glorify God and bless other people.

- [ ] Slowly repeat the prayer, "Christ is risen! He goes ahead of us into our group meeting" (*JOTS*, p. 112).

RESPONSIBILITIES IN MINISTRY (R STAGE)
Journey of the Soul Chapter 5 Summary

> **THEME**
> **WE GROW WHEN WE USE OUR GIFTS TO SERVE GOD AND BLESS PEOPLE.**

KEY SCRIPTURE
"Fan into flame the gift of God, which is in you through the laying on of my hands. For the Spirit God gave us does not make us timid, but gives us power, love and self-discipline." *2 Timothy 1:6-7*

TRAIL MARKERS: R STAGE (SEE FULL TABLE ON *JOTS*, P. 108)

3rd CHRIST stage

Age	13 to adult
Cognitive Development	Conventional and identifying with authority
Roadblock	False identity (believing lies and condemnations)
Grace	Joy gifts for serving God
Spiritual Disciplines	Service projects, expressing spiritual gifts and personality, books and classes on serving and leading, discovering identity in Christ, sharing the gospel, praying for others

FALSE IDENTITIES (OR LIES) (JOTS, PP. 97-98)
- "You are what you do."
- "You are what you have."
- "You are what people say about you."

THE JOY GIFTS (SEE DEFINITIONS ON JOTS, P. 100)
- Dream-awakener
- Truth-teller
- Includer
- Shepherd
- Teacher
- Servant
- Encourager
- Investor
- Leader
- Healer

KEY QUOTES
- "Because of [people in the R Stage] our world is a much better place" (JOTS, p. 94).
- "To bolster our confidence in the R Stage, we take on the beliefs and values of authority figures, experts, or friends, so our faith tends to be conventional or conformist (Prov. 22:6)" (JOTS, p. 95).
- "Organizations tend to eat the souls of their servants" (JOTS, pp. 95-96).
- "Whatever our age or stage, we can find blessings in following the example of our Lord Jesus who worked as a common laborer until he was thirty years old, and then even during his public ministry he washed dirty feet and cooked breakfast for his hungry friends (John 13:14-15; 21:12)" (JOTS, p. 102).
- Jesus' easy yoke is "perfectly sized for your personality and needs" (JOTS, p. 103).
- "The [CHRIST] stage we reach does not necessarily correlate with greater faith and fruitfulness — the measure of our life is love (Mark 12:30-31)" (JOTS, p. 104).
- "Like Elijah, in our service for God we may overwork, try too hard to meet everybody's needs, or neglect basic self-care. We're especially prone to this burnout path in the R Stage" (see 1 Kings 18-19; JOTS, p. 106).
- "Instead of working *for* God we can also learn to work *with* God" (JOTS, p. 110).

GROUP TIME

WELCOME (5 MINUTES)
- Greet everyone with a smile and enthusiasm and thank them for coming.
- Share your excitement to learn together about serving God and blessing people in the stage of Responsibilities in Ministry (or R Stage).
- Reinforce group guidelines like keeping shares brief, listening without giving advice, and confidentiality (*Leader Guide*, pp. 21-22).
- Ask someone who is willing to open in prayer.

FUN ACTIVITY (5 MINUTES)

> **TIP**
> Your joyful love for Jesus will help the group to bond as his servants.

- Invite everyone to join you and celebrate the joy of following Jesus and serving God.
- Lead them in skipping like a child around the room while exclaiming, "I'm the disciple Jesus loves! I'm the disciple Jesus loves! I'm the disciple Jesus loves!"

SCRIPTURE READING (5 MINUTES)
- Invite group members to read out loud a favorite Scripture for the R Stage (*JOTS*, p. 109).

INTRODUCE R STAGE (15 MINUTES)

> **TIP**
> Affirm the great value of people's talents and desires for serving God.

- Play one of the worship songs from the Soul Shepherding playlist "R Stage: Journey of the Soul" or encourage people to listen on their own (see journeyofthesoul.org).
- Share with your group this week's *JOTS* video on "Serving God" (see journeyofthesoul.org).

- Read the key Scripture for *JOTS* chapter five (see above) and comment briefly on why you like it.
- Read two or three of your favorite quotes from JOTS chapter five (see above) and comment briefly on why you like them.
- Ask the group, "What stood out to you about the R Stage in the journey with Jesus? Or maybe you have a question?"

> **TIP**
> Offer empathy for any stress, frustration, or discouragement people feel in their work or ministry.

SOUL TALK (30 MINUTES)

> **TIP**
> You may not have time for all the soul talk questions below. Choose the ones you believe are most helpful for your group.

1. *Optional*: What were your peak and pit this past week? How did you sense God's presence in these situations?

2. Which of the false identities or lies have you struggled with: I am what I do, I am what I have, I am what people say about me?

> **TIP**
> Cultivate and affirm people's trust in Jesus to guide and empower their leadership or service.

3. How does it feel to identify yourself as the disciple Jesus loves? What helps you to live that way?

4. Which joy gift(s) do you most enjoy using to serve others? How does this feel for you?

> **TIP**
> Affirm the "little" acts of care, kindness, or prayer that people offer as the greatest examples of ministry success.

5. Which of "Elijah's disciplines" of self-care do you most need in your life now? (e.g., sleep, healthy food, nature, physical touch, exercise, soul talk, being quiet and still, delegating tasks to others) (*JOTS*, pp. 105-107).

SOUL CARE PRACTICE (15 MINUTES)
- Invite anyone who wants to do so to share briefly about their experience last week with practicing what they're learning in group.
- Comment briefly on the value of quietly meditating on Scripture for growing in discipleship to Jesus.
- Prayerfully read the guided meditation on "Christ goes ahead of you," leaving quiet pauses after each part (*JOTS*, pp. 111-112).
- After the meditation invite people to share briefly on their thoughts or feelings during the experience.

SET UP NEXT MEETING (2 MINUTES)
Ask your group participants to:
- Read *Journey of the Soul* chapter six on "Through The Wall" (*JOTS*, p. 115).
- Experiment with the soul care practice on "Praying a Psalm of Lament" at the end of chapter six (*JOTS*, p. 138).
- Listen to the worship songs on the Soul Shepherding playlist, "The Wall: Journey of the Soul" (see journeyofthesoul.org).

CLOSING PRAYER (1 MINUTE)
- Ask someone who is willing to close the group with a short prayer.
- Or if time allows take prayer requests and ask group members to pray for each other.

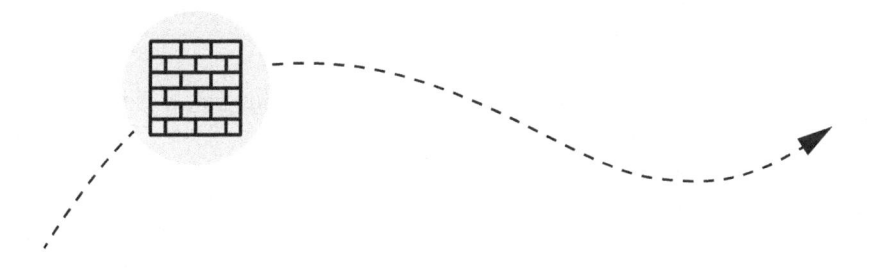

Week 4
THROUGH THE WALL

LEADER PREP
Overview

As we follow Jesus on the path of life we eventually come to The Wall in the middle of the progression of CHRIST stages (see chapter six in *JOTS*). It's not a stage but a transition from the First Half in our journey with Jesus to the Second Half. We lose our enthusiasm for reading the Bible, praying, attending church, or doing other spiritual activities. God may feel distant, unkind, allowing injustice, or even being mean. This session focuses on the wilderness time and what to do about it.

Some people in your group may be at The Wall and others will have experienced it before. Those who have not yet encountered The Wall may be scared by it. All of believers, whatever their stage of faith, experience trials and desolations that come and go. But it seems The Wall won't go away no matter how hard we pray. It doesn't feel like it, but at The Wall there is actually a blessed opportunity from God to learn to rest in Christ's grace and wait for the Spirit to open the gate to the path ahead. People in this painful and disorienting season especially need a guide and friends who offer patient empathy, gentle wisdom, and faithful prayers.

TO DO LIST

- Read *JOTS* chapter 6 and this leader guide.
- Watch the companion video "Through The Wall" and arrange to share it in group.
- Choose a song to share in group from the Soul Shepherding playlist "The Wall: Journey of the Soul."
- Pray for your group (see below).

Empathy

Some of your *JOTS* group members may be at The Wall and others will have experienced it in the past. In this season of disorientation and desolation people tend to isolate and shut down. This group is an opportune time for them to participate in a safe community with soul friends who help them to verbalize their questions and distress and gain faith to keep praying and seeking God — even though his face feels hidden. As a group leader your authentic devotion to Jesus, patient empathy, understanding of the CHRIST stages, and faithful prayers can be a lifeline to connect people at The Wall with Jesus.

PRAYER POINTS

- Ask Jesus to lead the group to be emotionally safe and spiritually encouraging for each participant.

- Pray for group members who are at The Wall or experiencing another trial to have strength to persevere with Jesus.

- Imagine Jesus on the cross as you pray for your group, "The Lord is our shepherd, we lack nothing" (*JOTS*, p. 140).

THROUGH THE WALL
Journey of the Soul Chapter 6 Summary

> **THEME**
> **SPIRITUAL DRYNESS OR GETTING STUCK IS A HIDDEN OPPORTUNITY FOR DEEPER GROWTH AND JOY.**

KEY SCRIPTURE
"Even though I walk through the darkest valley, I will fear no evil, for you are with me." *Psalm 23:4*

TRAIL MARKERS: THE WALL (SEE FULL TABLE ON *JOTS*, P. 136)

Transition between First Half and Second Half	
Age	18+
Cognitive Development	Questioning authority
Roadblock	Distrusting God
Grace	God's empathy
Spiritual Disciplines	Receiving care, working less, enjoying God's blessings, napping, praying Psalms of lament

TWO SPIRITUALITIES (SEE FULL LIST ON *JOTS*, P. 123)
- First Half (C, H, and R Stages) vs. Second Half (I, S, and T Stages)
- Black and white vs. gray
- Security in blessings vs. security in God's kingdom

- Outward behavior vs. inward character
- Minimize emotions vs. empathy
- Bible programs vs. experiences with living Word
- Personal abilities vs. Presence of Holy Spirit

SIX TYPES OF WALLS
1. **Burnout**: from overworking
2. **Spiritual burnout**: compulsive spirituality or compassion fatigue
3. **Blowout**: moral failing
4. **Personal crisis**: disease, grief
5. **Faith crisis**: disbelief, cynicism
6. **Dark Night of the Soul**: ongoing spiritual dryness

KEY QUOTES
- "We're likely to encounter The Wall after we leave home (literally or symbolically) and at least once more later in life" (JOTS, p. 117).
- "Our situation at The Wall is like the Chinese word for 'crisis,' which combines the characters for 'danger' and 'opportunity'" (JOTS, p. 118).
- "The Israelites of old [got] through the sea-wall on dry ground by trusting and following Yahweh's unseen footprints (Ps. 77:19). They trusted the Lord as their Way Maker" (JOTS, p. 119).
- "The two halves of life are like two different soul containers or spiritualities . . . there is often misunderstanding, distrust, or strife between the two" (JOTS, p. 122).
- "Tragically, we may become resigned to a faith that lacks intimacy and vitality" (JOTS, p. 125).
- "At The Wall we're susceptible to distrust God because we feel we've outgrown what our parents, church, or other spiritual leaders taught us" (JOTS, p. 125).
- "'Necessary suffering' now helps us prevent 'unnecessary suffering' later" (Carl Jung; JOTS, p. 127).
- "The passageway through The Wall is to 'make every effort to enter [God's] rest,' opening our hearts to the loving Word of God and to one another (Heb. 4:11–13)" (JOTS, p. 133).
- "Psalms 22 and 23 give language for the disorientation and distress we feel at The Wall (and in other trials) and inspire our prayers of faith so we can reorient to the loving presence of our Shepherd-Christ" (JOTS, p. 139).

GROUP TIME

WELCOME (5 MINUTES)
- Greet everyone with a smile and enthusiasm and thank them for coming.
- Share your interest to learn together about getting through The Wall of spiritual dryness and faith challenges in the journey of discipleship to Jesus.
- Remind everyone of group guidelines that need reinforcing, like keeping shares brief, listening without giving advice, and confidentiality (*Leader Guide*, pp. 21-22).
- Ask someone who is willing to open in prayer.

SCRIPTURE READING (5 MINUTES)

> **TIP**
> Point out that many men and women in the Bible struggled with spiritual distress, disorientation, or dryness.

- Invite group members to read out loud a favorite Scripture for The Wall (*JOTS*, p. 137).

INTRODUCE THE WALL (15 MINUTES)
- Play one of the worship songs from the Soul Shepherding playlist "The Wall: Journey of the Soul" or encourage people to listen on their own (see journeyofthesoul.org).
- Share with your group this week's *JOTS* video "Through the Wall" (see journeyofthesoul.org).
- Read the key Scripture for *JOTS* chapter six (see above) and comment briefly on why you like it.
- Read two or three of your favorite quotes from *JOTS* chapter six (see above) and comment briefly on why you like them.

> **TIP**
> Explain to your group that being at The Wall is not their fault — it's the Lord's invitation into deeper awareness and intimacy.

- Briefly discuss the Consolations and Desolations Timeline diagram (*JOTS*, p. 46).
- Ask the group, "What stood out to you about The Wall in the journey with Jesus? Or maybe you have a question?"

> **TIP**
> If someone is in a dark valley affirm their persevering faith and love.

SOUL TALK (35 MINUTES)

> **TIP**
> You may not have time for all the soul talk questions below. Choose the ones you believe are most helpful for your group.

1. *Optional*: What were your peak and pit this past week? How did you sense God's presence in these situations?

2. How is it helpful to you to understand The Wall as a transition season from the First Half to the Second Half of the CHRIST stages?

3. Which of the six types of walls have you or someone close to you encountered? (e.g., burnout, compassion fatigue, moral blowout, personal crisis, faith crisis, or Dark Night of feeling far from God). Briefly describe this.

> **TIP**
> Help people verbalize their spiritual questions or doubts and offer empathy.

4. What person in the Bible encourages you that you can break through tough times? How do you relate to their story?

5. Who is someone that has given you empathy and grace in trials? How has this helped you to trust Jesus?

SOUL CARE PRACTICE (15 MINUTES)

> **TIP**
> Give hope that expressing emotion and cultivating longing for God in the Inner Journey stage (discussed next) helps us respond to the Spirit of Jesus guiding us through The Wall.

- Invite anyone who wants to do so to share briefly about their experience last week with practicing what they're learning in group.
- Comment briefly on how the Psalms of lament help us to pray through emotional distress.
- Read out loud the "Psalm 22-23 Meditation" which features key verses to receive Jesus' ministry at the cross (*JOTS*, pp. 139-140).
- After the meditation invite people to share briefly on their thoughts or feelings during the experience.

SET UP NEXT MEETING (2 MINUTES)
Ask your group participants to:
- Read *Journey of the Soul* chapter seven on "Your Inner Journey" (*JOTS*, p. 143).
- Experiment with the soul care practice on "Enthrallment with Jesus" at the end of chapter seven (*JOTS*, p. 162).
- Listen to the worship songs on the Soul Shepherding playlist, "I Stage: Journey of the Soul" (see journeyofthesoul.org).

CLOSING PRAYER (1 MINUTE)
- Ask someone who is willing to close the group with a short prayer.
- Or if time allows take prayer requests and ask group members to pray for each other.

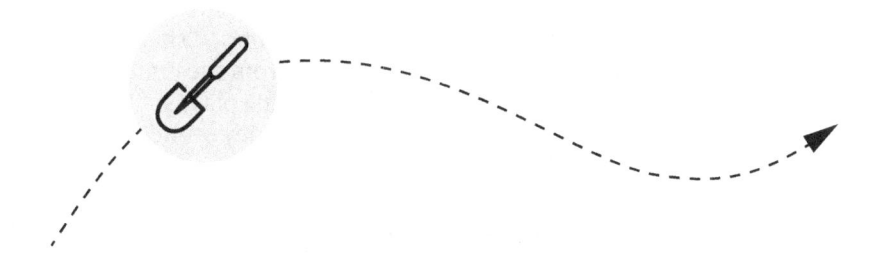

Week 5
YOUR INNER JOURNEY

LEADER PREP
Overview

We've been learning about the progression of emotional and spiritual growth for apprentices of Christ. This session goes deeper into the feelings side of faith by exploring the Inner Journey (or the I Stage). The I Stage is the heart of the CHRIST stages. It's also the soul pivot stage. It can be a time of wonderful blessings, spiritual renewal, intimacy with Jesus and others, and great joy. But before that we may have to deal with faith questions, doubts, emotional distress, burnout, spiritual dryness, or other trials. Many Christians do not experience Inner Journey spirituality. For those who do it's usually not until after age forty.

In your small group there might be some people that are approaching or currently in the Inner Journey and need help understanding their experience and receiving God's grace. The Holy Spirit can use this material and your shepherding to help people in your group get unstuck at The Wall and experience the deeper life of the I Stage.

TO DO LIST

☐ Read *JOTS* chapter 7 and this leader guide.

☐ Pray for your group (see below).

☐ Watch the companion video "Your Inner Journey" and arrange to share it in group.

☐ Choose a song to share in group from the Soul Shepherding playlist "I Stage: Journey of the Soul."

☐ Determine if your group wants to end after the sixth meeting or schedule a half-day retreat or bonus meeting to make and share their Journey Maps. Make plans accordingly.

Empathy

The I Stage is a tender phase of discipleship to the Lord. Your group members need your empathy and prayers as they learn to feel and express more sadness, spiritual longing, and affection for Jesus and his Abba. Also your story of how God met you at The Wall can encourage their faith. If they persevere in the I Stage by wrestling through their questions, being emotionally honest with God and soul friends, and using a wise program of spiritual disciplines then eventually they're likely to experience a wonderful spiritual renewal of intimacy with God and other people.

PRAYER POINTS

☐ Ask Jesus to help people share emotions and give empathy.

☐ Pray for everyone to grow in a deeper experience of Jesus and Abba's love.

☐ Repeat the Breath Prayer, "Abba, I belong to you." Then pray this for your group members (*JOTS*, p. 159).

YOUR INNER JOURNEY
Journey of the Soul Chapter 7 Summary

> **THEME**
> **WE EXPERIENCE SPIRITUAL RENEWAL THROUGH EMPATHY, EMOTIONAL GROWTH, AND LONGING FOR GOD.**

KEY SCRIPTURE
"Because we are his children, God has sent the Spirit of his Son into our hearts, prompting us to call out, 'Abba, Father.'" *Galatians 4:6 NLT*

TRAIL MARKERS: I STAGE (SEE FULL TABLE ON *JOTS*, P. 160)

4th CHRIST Stage

Age	18+ (usually 30+, if ever)
Cognitive Development	Self-reflection and intrinsic beliefs
Roadblock	Denying emotions, needs, or problems
Grace	Deeper experiences of God's love
Spiritual Disciplines	Praying the Psalms, empathy, Lectio Divina, quiet prayer, reading devotional classics

MIRRORING JESUS' EMOTIONS (JOTS, PP. 149-151)
Jesus felt all the emotions that we do and seeing this can help us be aware and loving with our emotions. Here are some of the feeling words used in the Bible to describe Jesus' experiences:
- Anxiety
- Anger
- Shame
- Sadness
- Pain
- Surprise
- Curiosity
- Hope
- Confidence
- Love
- Joy
- Peace

TERMS FOR DEEPER EXPERIENCES (JOTS, PP. 152-155)
- Walking in the Spirit
- The life of faith
- Death to the self-life
- Being filled with the Spirit
- The baptism of the Holy Spirit
- Entire sanctification
- Whole-hearted consecration
- Overcoming power
- Pure love

KEY QUOTES
- "[In] the I Stage... we work through the limitations of our earlier experiences with family and church, try on new spiritual values, and express a more authentic spirituality" (JOTS, p. 145).
- "By being emotionally honest with God and trustworthy people in the I Stage we receive more of the Holy Spirit's inner healing and re-forming" (Ja. 5:16; JOTS, p. 145).
- "If we don't integrate our spiritual and emotional growth, we get stuck at The Wall and stop growing" (JOTS, p. 148).
- "We're prone to deny the emotions that are distressing, but that banishes them into an unconsious region of our body where they can become toxic and cause sickness, depression, anxiety, addiction, cynicism, isolation, or destructive conflicts with people (e.g., Psalm 32:3-4)" (JOTS, p. 150).
- "Learning to feel your emotions softens your heart for [God's] grace" (JOTS, p. 152).
- "Do you know that Abba God is very fond of you? Treats you tenderly? Really likes you?!" (see Gal. 4:6; Rom. 8:15; JOTS, p. 155).
- "When we find that we're not longing for God, we can learn to *long* to long for God. We can nuture affectionate reverence for Jesu and Abba through heart-awakening disciplines" (JOTS, p. 159).
- "Enthralling our minds with God is the *primary* objective in Dallas Willard's 'Curriculum for Christlikeness'" (JOTS, p. 162).

WEEK 5: **YOUR INNER JOURNEY**

GROUP TIME

WELCOME (5 MINUTES)
- Greet everyone with a smile and enthusiasm and thank them for coming.
- Share your excitement to learn together about the Inner Journey (or the I Stage) for growing in emotional and spiritual health with Jesus.
- Reinforce any group guidelines as needed (*Leader Guide*, pp. 21-22).
- Ask someone who is willing to open in prayer.

SCRIPTURE READING (5 MINUTES)
- Invite group members to read out loud a favorite Scripture for the I Stage (*JOTS*, p. 161).

INTRODUCE THE I STAGE (15 MINUTES)
- Play one of the worship songs from the Soul Shepherding playlist "I Stage: Journey of the Soul" or encourage people to listen on their own (see journeyofthesoul.org).
- Share with your group this week's *JOTS* video on "Your Inner Journey" (see journeyofthesoul.org).
- Read the key Scripture for *JOTS* chapter seven (see above) and comment briefly on why you like it.

> **TIP**
> Practice I Stage spirituality by expressing your affection for Jesus.

- Read two or three of your favorite quotes from *JOTS* chapter seven (see above) and comment briefly on why you like them.
- Briefly discuss the Growth in Christ diagram (*JOTS*, p. 148).
- Ask the group, "What stood out to you about the I Stage in the journey with Jesus? Or maybe you have a question?"

> **TIP**
> Practice I stage spirituality by sharing a personal struggle with emotion. This gives group members permission to be vulnerable also.

SOUL TALK (35 MINUTES)

> **TIP**
> You may not have time for all the soul talk questions below. Choose the ones you believe are most helpful for your group.

1. *Optional*: What were your peak and pit this past week? How did you sense God's presence in these situations?

> **TIP**
> If someone in your group seems to be denying emotion be gentle so you don't mobilize increased resistance.

2. How does it help you to see Bible stories with Jesus experiencing the full range of negative and positive emotions? (e.g., anxiety, anger, shame, sadness, pain, suprise, curiosity, hope, confidence, love, joy, and peace).

3. What's your response to the spiritual mother Jean Guyon saying "We all have been called to the depths of Christ"?

> **TIP**
> Mirror group members' emotions that are just under the surface of their awareness (don't go too deep) to help them find words for their experience and feel cared for.

4. What memories or feelings surfaced for you when you reflected on the parable of reaching the summit of the mountain?

5. How might it help you to use "hungry-heart disciplines" like imagining yourself with Jesus in Gospel stories, fasting and feasting on Scripture, or reading classic Christian devotional books to cultivate your intimacy with Jesus? (for the whole list see *JOTS*, p. 159).

SOUL CARE PRACTICE (15 MINUTES)
- Invite anyone who wants to do so to share briefly about their experience last week with practicing what they're learning in group.

> **TIP**
> Listen carefully for people's heart-longings for God and verbally affirm them.

- Prayerfully read the Scripture meditation on "Enthrallment with Jesus" which features key verses form Colossians. Then allow thirty seconds of silence at the end (*JOTS*, pp. 162-165).
- After the meditation invite people to share briefly on their thoughts or feelings during the experience.

SET UP NEXT MEETING (2 MINUTES)
Ask your group participants to:
- Read *Journey of the Soul* chapter eight on "Spirit-Led Ministry" and chapter nine on "Transforming Union" (*JOTS*, p. 167 and p. 193).
- Experiment with the soul care practice on "Centering in Christ" (*JOTS*, p. 189) or "Consecration Prayer" (*JOTS*, p. 212).
- Listen to the worship songs on the Soul Shepherding playlists, "S Stage: Journey of the Soul" and "T Stage: Journey of the Soul" (see journeyofthesoul.org).

CLOSING PRAYER (1 MINUTE)
- Ask someone who is willing to close the group with a short prayer.
- Or if time allows take prayer requests and ask group members to pray for each other.

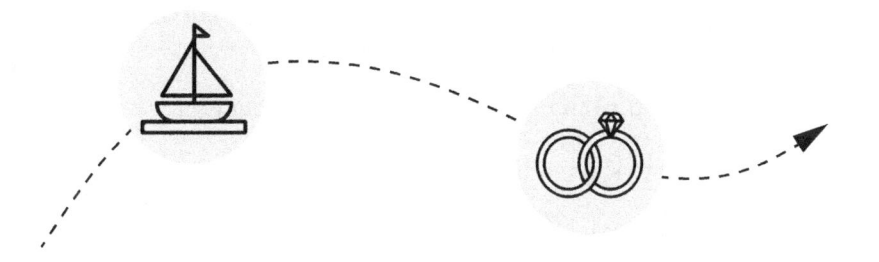

Week 6
SPACIOUS PLACES

LEADER PREP
Overview

Our journey of growing emotionally and spiritually in the way of Jesus culminates in the last two CHRIST stages: Spirit-Led Ministry (the S Stage) and Transforming Union (the T Stage). Most of the people in your group are probably not in the S or T Stages and there may not be anyone who is. Nonetheless, everyone can learn from the spirituality of these stages: hearing God's voice, persevering in trials, living and working in Jesus' easy yoke, offering our wounds in God's service, practicing God's presence, and extending compassion to all people. As a group leader you can make a space for the less mature and the more mature to be in relationship, following the Lord Jesus together.

TO DO LIST

- [ ] Read *JOTS* chapters 8 and 9 and this leader guide.

- [ ] Watch the companion video "Spacious Places" and arrange to share it in group.

- [ ] Choose a song to share in group from the Soul Shepherding playlist "S Stage: Journey of the Soul."

- [ ] Pray for your group (see below).

Empathy

It's important to understand and accept people in different CHRIST stages. In the Second Half of the journey people tend to become more open-minded, inclusive, quiet, process-oriented, grace-giving, and free. It's often hard for them to find a place in church. At the same time, those in the First Half may feel intimidated by them. Your role is to offer empathy, respect, and spiritual growth opportunities for people in every stage.

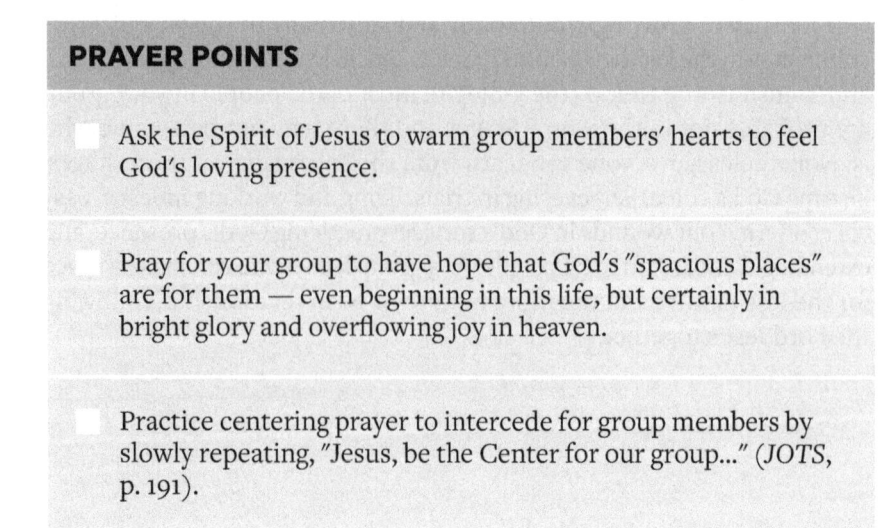

PRAYER POINTS

- [ ] Ask the Spirit of Jesus to warm group members' hearts to feel God's loving presence.

- [ ] Pray for your group to have hope that God's "spacious places" are for them — even beginning in this life, but certainly in bright glory and overflowing joy in heaven.

- [ ] Practice centering prayer to intercede for group members by slowly repeating, "Jesus, be the Center for our group..." (*JOTS*, p. 191).

WEEK 6: **SPACIOUS PLACES**

SPIRIT-LED MINISTRY
Journey of the Soul Chapter 8 Summary

> **THEME**
> **OUR GREATEST JOY AND IMPACT IS TO ACT WITH THE PRESENCE AND POWER OF THE SPIRIT TO SERVE OTHERS.**

KEY SCRIPTURE
"Come to me... I'll show you how to take a real rest. Walk with me and work with me — watch how I do it. Learn the unforced rhythms of grace."
Matthew 11:28-30 MSG

TRAIL MARKERS: S STAGE (SEE FULL TABLE ON *JOTS*, P. 187)

	5th CHRIST Stage
Age	Usually 40+ (if ever)
Cognitive Development	Integrating paradoxes and transcending limits
Roadblock	Dark Night of the Soul (prolonged spiritual dryness)
Grace	Surprise blessings to share
Spiritual Disciplines	Watching and praying to act with Holy Spirit, abandoning outcomes to God, listening to God, abiding in prayer for self and others, secrecy

GPS FOR HEARING GOD (SEE DIAGRAM ON *JOTS*, P. 177)
- God's Word
- Providence
- Spirit impressions

SIGNS OF GOD'S VOICE (*JOTS*, P.P 178-181)
- Consistent with the Bible
- Calm authority
- Exalted peace and sweet reasonableness
- Gentle like the Spirit of Jesus
- Surprises you
- Offers a world of meaning
- Brings clarity
- Imprints into your memory
- Produces a living spark of faith
- Inspires you to worship God
- Humbles you
- Turns you away from worldly things

KEY QUOTES
- "At the S Stage we're learning to minister to others out of the overflow of God's love — we're blessed to be a blessing to others (2 Cor. 9:14; Phil. 1:9 NLT)" (*JOTS*, p. 169).
- "When God speaks to us . . . we're simply receiving into our mind thoughts, feelings, or images, as was the case for Peter on the rooftop (Acts 10:9-21)" (*JOTS*, p. 179).
- "Teresa indicates that a genuine word from the Lord will typically surprise us, offer a world of meaning, bring clarity, imprint into our memory, and produce a living spark of faith..." (*JOTS*, p. 180).
- "Henri Nouwen taught that wounded healers in the way of Jesus do not give analysis, advice, fixing, or reassurance. Instead, they give empathy by listening. Surprisingly, sometimes they also verbalize their own weaknesses and brokenness to the people they teach or care for" (*JOTS*, p. 182).
- "Often anxiety is a sign that we're relying not on the Holy Spirit but on our own attempts to perform or feel in control" (*JOTS*, p. 183).
- "Jesus' easy yoke is not an easy life — it's an easy way of doing hard things" (Gal. 4:6; Rom. 8:15; *JOTS*, p. 185).
- "[We can learn] to be quiet in 'the Silence which is the source of sound' and *behold Christ transfigured in our hearts*" (*JOTS*, p. 191).

TRANSFORMING UNION
Journey of the Soul Chapter 9 Summary

> **THEME**
> **OUR JOURNEY OF THE SOUL CULMINATES WITH BEING UNITED IN THE LOVE OF JESUS CHRIST.**

KEY SCRIPTURE
"Christ is all and is in all." *Colossians 3:11*

TRAIL MARKERS: T STAGE (SEE FULL TABLE ON *JOTS*, P. 210)

6th CHRIST Stage

Age	Usually 60+ (if ever)
Cognitive Development	Universalizing compassion for all
Roadblock	Diminishing Jesus Christ
Grace	Practicing God's presence
Spiritual Disciplines	Turning activity into prayer, contemplative prayer, appreciating the Trinity, staying engaged in church, blessing those who mistreat you

THE FOUR WATERS (*JOTS*, PP. 205-207)

1st Water	Using a bucket at a well	C & H Stages
2nd Water	Building a waterwheel	R Stage
No Water	Running out of water	The Wall
3rd Water	Creating an outflowing stream from a spring	I Stage
4th Water	Praying and God sends rain or mist	S & T Stages

KEY QUOTES

- "[In the T Stage] you have compassion for *all* people and welcome whoever you can into your expanding community" (*JOTS*, p. 195).
- "Martin Luther King Jr. (1929-1968) was [in the T Stage as] an ordinary pastor in Atlanta, Georgia, who rose up to defend African Americans against racial injustice" (*JOTS*, p. 196).
- "In the later stages of faith we set our affections on Christ above, deny ourselves worldly pleasures and honors, and live to love all people for his sake (Col. 3:1-17)" (*JOTS*, p. 201).
- "The Son graces us, the Father loves us, and the Spirit companions us... We become the Trinity's temple for others to experience God's presence (2 Cor. 13:14)" (*JOTS*, p. 199).
- "[A.W. Tozer] says Christian mysticism is being 'quietly, deeply, and sometimes almost ecstatically aware of the Presence of God in [our] own nature and in the world around [us]'" (*JOTS*, pp. 200-201).
- "If you long for intimacy with Jesus, enjoy contemplative prayer, and see the Holy Mystery in all things and all people... You may be persecuted by religious people" (*JOTS*, p. 201).
- "*We're marrying contemplative prayer and compassionate action.* This requires developing bodily habits for tuning in to and depending on the Breath of Life" (*JOTS*, p. 209).

WEEK 6: **SPACIOUS PLACES**

GROUP TIME

> **TIP**
> While you're talking pause occasionally to smile and appreciate the Spirit of Jesus who is present to minister to your friends.

WELCOME (5 MINUTES)
- Greet everyone with a smile and enthusiasm. Thank them for joining you on this journey.
- Share your excitement to learn together about the last two CHRIST stages of Spirit-Led Ministry (or the S Stage) and Transforming Union (or the T Stage).
- Reinforce any group guidelines as needed (*Leader Guide*, pp. 21-22).
- Ask someone who is willing to open in prayer.

SCRIPTURE READING (5 MINUTES)

> **TIP**
> Ask your group to leave a quiet pause of about ten seconds after each verse is read. People in the I, S, or T stages will especially appreciate this.

- Invite group members to read out loud a favorite Scripture for the S Stage (*JOTS*, p. 188).
- Invite group members to read out loud a favorite Scripture for the T Stage (*JOTS*, p. 211).

INTRODUCE THE S & T STAGES (15 MINUTES)
- Play one of the worship songs from the Soul Shepherding playlists "S Stage: Journey of the Soul" or "T Stage: Journey of the Soul" or encourage people to listen on their own (see journeyofthesoul.org).
- Share with your group this week's *JOTS* video on "Higher Places" (see journeyofthesoul.org).
- Read the key Scriptures for *JOTS* chapters eight and nine (see above) and comment briefly on why you like them.
- Read two or three of your favorite quotes from *JOTS* chapters eight and nine (see above) and comment briefly on why you like them.

- Ask the group, "What stood out to you about the S and T Stages in the journey with Jesus? Or maybe you have a question?"

> **TIP**
> Tell the group that the living Christ is present to listen and emotionally hold each person. As you listen, join Christ's ministry of empathy.

SOUL TALK (35 MINUTES)

> **TIP**
> You may not have time for all the soul talk questions below. Choose the ones you believe are most helpful for your group.

1. *Optional*: What were your peak and pit this past week? How did you sense God's presence in these situations?

> **TIP**
> Be generous with your empathy and grace for anyone in a trial or Dark Night as they may feel shame or fear.

2. Which distinguishing marks of a genuine word or vision from God are most helpful to you?

3. What does it look like for you to do your work or ministry in Jesus' easy yoke (Matt. 11:28-30) or as a wounded healer (2 Cor. 1:3-7)?

> **TIP**
> While you listen to group members share, shoot up silent little arrow prayers for them like, "Jesus care for my friend."

4. How does it feel if you relate to God as a Trinity of Father, Son, and Spirit with each one putting a spotlight of love and glory on the other two?

5. What's your experience with contemplative prayer that's quiet and uses few words or seeks to simply be in God's presence?

SOUL CARE PRACTICE (15 MINUTES)

> **TIP**
> For people who feel distracted, antsy, or anxious in quiet prayer it's helpful for you to verbalize this and offer empathy.

- Invite anyone who wants to do so to share briefly about their experience last week with practicing what they're learning in group.
- Read out loud the excerpt from the Quaker Thomas Kelly, "We feel the pull of many obligations..." Then share the prayer, "Jesus, be the Center."
- Lead the group in a Scripture meditation with quiet prayer on "Jesus be the Center" (*JOTS*, p. 191).
- After the meditation invite people to share briefly on their thoughts or feelings during the experience.

BONUS: SET UP JOURNEY MAP EXPERIENCE (5 MINUTES)
Ask your group members to:
- Schedule a half day retreat or bonus meeting for everyone to make and share their Journey Map of experiences in the CHRIST stages and The Wall. Or people can do this on their own or with a partner (*JOTS*, p. 219-220).
- Read *Journey of the Soul* chapter ten on "Friends on the Journey" (*JOTS*, p. 215).

> **TIP**
> If this is the last group meeting thank and affirm group members for their participation.

CLOSING PRAYER (1 MINUTE)
- Ask someone who is willing to close the group with a short prayer.
- Or if time allows take prayer requests and ask group members to pray for each other.

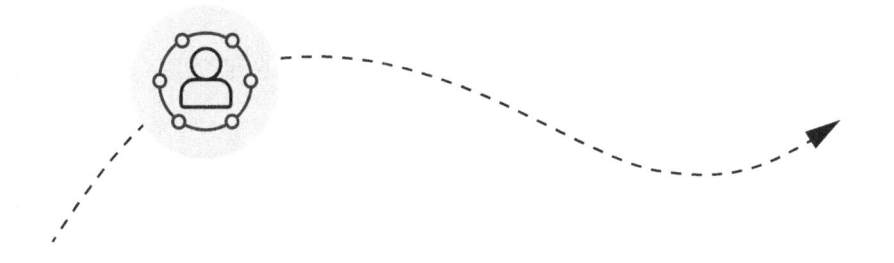

Bonus Group or Half-Day Retreat
MAKING A JOURNEY MAP

LEADER PREP
Overview

Making a Journey Map is an incredibly helpful spiritual tool. Noticing our personal experiences in the CHRIST stages and The Wall gives us a new framework to understand the ups and downs in our discipleship to Jesus. We can better see our developing faith and the different expressions of God's grace in our life. This landscape vista can provide much-needed clarity, peace, and confidence. We're learning better how to cooperate with the Spirit of Jesus in the situations of our lives.

Your group members can choose to work on their Journey Maps during a small group meeting, as part of a retreat, with a friend, or on their own. *JOTS* chapter 10 and this section of the *Leader Guide* give instructions for this exercise. To prepare for this group meeting, or as part of a retreat, people may want to spend some time in quiet prayer to reflect on their journey with Jesus. The section below on "Suggestions For Solitude With Jesus" gives guidance.

TO DO LIST

- [ ] Read *JOTS* chapter 10 and this leader guide.
- [ ] Prepare a room with large tables and the supplies for making the Journey Maps.
- [ ] Watch the companion video "Making a Journey Map" and arrange to share it in group.
- [ ] Pray for your group.

Empathy

When group members plot their journey through the CHRIST stages they will likely be tempted to compare themselves with others and may fall into shame or pride. It's important to help people remember that the measure of our virtue is not our stage but our love for God and neighbor. You have the opportunity to set a powerful example for people to appreciate and learn from one another's different stories and stages so they learn and grow in the love of Christ.

PRAYER POINTS

- [ ] Ask Jesus to guide everyone in making their Journey Map.
- [ ] Pray for group members to identify their consolations (peaks) and desolations (pits) in their journey and key insights God has given them.
- [ ] Abide in prayer imagining each group member as consecrated to the Lord.

FRIENDS ON THE JOURNEY
Journey of the Soul Chapter 10 Summary

> **THEME**
> **UNDERSTANDING AND SHARING OUR STORIES OF FAITH FACILITATES TRUE COMMUNITY.**

KEY SCRIPTURE
Jesus said, "I have come to give you everything in abundance, more than you expect — life in its fullness until you overflow!" *John 10:10 TPT*

JOURNEY MAP SUPPLIES
- Poster board or large, heavy weight sheets of paper (with extras)
- Paper for notes
- Pencils, colored pencils, colored markers
- Erasers
- Different colored small sticky notes
- Scissors

GROUP PREPARATION
Recruit group members to help you with this meeting:
- Secure a retreat space or meeting room
- Gather or purchase needed supplies
- Purchase snacks, drinks, and possibly lunch or dinner
- Arrange the room with large tables (for work space)
- Set out all the supplies at a central location
- Prepare to stream music from the Journey of the Soul playlists

KEY QUOTES
- "[In Hebrews 11] faith does not mean believing for and receiving miraculous answers to prayer — it's persevering in the ups and downs of life to keep loving God and people because you trust that the Lord is beautiful, good, just, and loving all the time" (*JOTS*, p. 215).
- "[Abraham] experienced consolation and desolation, failure and success, and through it all he had the opportunity to grow spiritually" (*JOTS*, pp. 215-216).
- "Often we have trouble connecting with people who are two CHRIST stages apart from us. An important lesson from Abraham's life is that

true community includes being in relationship with people who are in different stages of the journey than you are" (*JOTS*, p. 217).
- "Friends can offer empathy and encouragement to one another to understand their current stage and follow Jesus in it" (*JOTS*, p. 217).
- "Mapping your journey with Jesus at different ages helps you to better appreciate God's presence and activity in your life. It helps you to track your journey through the CHRIST stages of emotional and spiritual growth with their consolations, desolations, and life lessons" (*JOTS*, p. 219).
- "Jesus says to us, 'Come with me by yourselves to a quiet place and get some rest' (Mark 6:31)" (*JOTS*, p. 219).

ABRAHAM'S JOURNEY MAP (SEE FULL TABLE ON *JOTS*, P. 216)

C	Called by God to promised land
H	Builds altar to God
R	Gives tithes to Melchizedek
Wall	Infertility and marriage problems
I	Repents of lying habit then promised son is born
Wall	Sacrifices son to God
I	Grieves wife's death
S	Trains servant to hear God and find son's wife
T	Leaves legacy of blessing and faith in God

GROUP TIME

> **TIP**
> You can adjust the activities or schedule for your meeting depending upon how much time you have and the needs of your group.

WELCOME (5 MINUTES)
- Greet everyone with a smile and enthusiasm. Thank them for joining you in this retreat day (or bonus meeting).
- Share your enthusiasm about being together on retreat to make and share your Journey Maps.
- Reinforce any group guidelines as needed (*Leader Guide*, pp. 21-22).
- Pray with thanks to God for the group's journey and ask Jesus to be the Retreat Leader (or Group Leader). Pray that everyone comes to understand the whole picture of their life's journey through the CHRIST stages.

SCRIPTURE READING (5 MINUTES)
- Invite group members to read out loud a favorite Scripture on the journey of faith from Hebrews 11 (e.g., insights in vv. 1, 8, 39-40 or faith examples throughout the chapter).

INTRODUCE "FRIENDS ON THE JOURNEY" (15 MINUTES)
- Play one or more favorite worship songs from the Soul Shepherding playlists for *Journey of the Soul* or encourage people to listen on their own (see journeyofthesoul.org)
- Share with your group the JOTS video on "Making a Journey Map" (see journeyofthesoul.org)
- Read the key Scripture for JOTS chapter ten (see above) and comment briefly on why you like it.
- Read two or three of your favorite quotes from JOTS chapter ten (see above) and comment briefly on why you like them.
- Ask the group, "What stood out to you about the journey of faith? (e.g., Abraham's Journey Map on the left). Or maybe you have a question?"

INSTRUCTIONS FOR JOURNEY MAPS (5 MINUTES)

> **TIP**
> If you need to shorten your meeting ask group members to make their Journey Maps on their own and bring them to the last meeting.

Have everyone sit at tables with work space and explain these steps:
1. Gather several large sheets of paper, a pencil, and an eraser (to make adjustments). You may also want colored pencils or markers and/or sticky notes of different colors.
2. Pray for the Holy Spirit to illuminate your memory and give you insights.
3. At the top of your map, divide your history into ages or life periods.
4. For each age, plot key consolation events (e.g., God's blessings).
5. For each age, plot key desolation events (e.g., lack of blessings).
6. For each age, plot key spiritual insights you discovered.
7. Plot your CHRIST stages. (You may not have experienced some yet).

MAKING JOURNEY MAPS (2 HOURS)
- Answer people's questions as needed
- Invite them to take breaks for bathroom or food
- Turn on the *JOTS* playlists to encourage fun and socializing!

SOUL TALK (45 MINUTES)

> **TIP**
> Sharing Journey Maps can be done as a whole group or with a partner or triad. Breaking the group into clusters allows more time for people to share.

> **TIP**
> Invite group members to take turns using their Journey Maps as a visual aid while answering the questions. Share first to set a model of authenticity and being brief.

1. What are two seasons of consolation from your journey with Jesus? Briefly summarize these.

2. What are two seasons of desolation from your journey with Jesus? Briefly summarize these.

3. Which CHRIST stage are you currently experiencing and what is this like for you?

4. What are two key life lessons the Lord has taught you in your inner journey?

SOUL CARE PRACTICE (20 MINUTES)

> **TIP**
> You may want to have one or more group members offer an affirmation or prayer for each person right after they share their map.

- Lead a time of group affirmations or prayers in which each person's personal journey and growth are appreciated and celebrated.

CLOSING PRAYER (1 MINUTE)
- Give thanks to God for your group and everyone's experience of community and growth in discipleship to Jesus.
- If time allows you can take prayer requests and ask group members to pray briefly for each other.

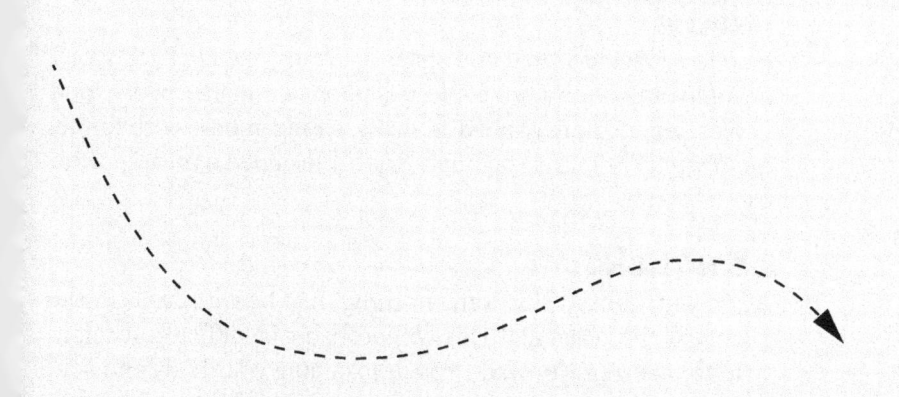

SUGGESTIONS FOR SOLITUDE WITH JESUS

To prepare for making your Journey Map it'd be helpful if you're able to spend some time in solitude and silence with Jesus. It's valuable for your spiritual and emotional growth to periodically set aside a few hours or more for training, but even a few minutes of quiet prayer makes a postive difference. You're making space to reflect on your life journey with Jesus and hear God's voice. Here are some ideas to get you started.

1. PREPARE

Bring to your solitude whatever will help you to be with Jesus in a personal, interactive way. Probably you'll want your Bible, journal, and pen. If you'll be outside you may need walking shoes, a chair, sun protection, jacket or blanket, and water. You may need a lunch or snacks or you might choose to fast. Also you could bring art supplies, a favorite devotional book, a musical instrument, or worship music.

2 UNPLUG
Plan to set aside a time and space for Jesus in which you won't be interrupted by other people, cell phones, e-mails, media, loud noises, etc. (You may need to make arrangements with family members or others.) You might go to a secluded nature sport or a quiet room.

3 DO NOTHING!
Begin your solitude by doing nothing. Just be with Jesus in the silence with no agenda. This will probably be difficult! It might help to take a prayer walk. You are training your body and soul to listen to the word of the Lord: "Be still and know that I am God" (Psalm 46:10). With practice you can live your daily life in Jesus' easy yoke (Matthew 11:25-30), free of hurry, worry, and selfish ambition.

4 LET GO
You may be hoping to have a special time with God, hear a message from him, or to accomplish something important — release your desires to the Lord. You may be anxious about your work, a loved one, or a personal matter — put each concern into the Father's hands. Ask Jesus to lead you in this time and then be open to whatever he has for you, trusting that it is good even if it doesn't feel good. You may feel refreshed by God or distress may surface. You may be encouraged or challenged. Remember that *God is just as present in your desolations as your consolations.*

5 REST
What would you enjoy doing with Jesus? He is your Best Friend and he likes being with you! Probably you don't want to do a major Bible study or lots of reading. Set aside any concerns for loved ones or your ministry until the last part of your solitude. Instead of trying to accomplish projects, simply pray from your heart, perhaps meditating on a Psalm or Gospel story. If you're tired you may need to take a nap. Go ahead — Jesus took naps! This will help you to be refreshed and attentive to God.

6 RE-FOCUS
In prayer everyone struggles with distracting thoughts — don't feel bad about it. When your mind wanders offer the distraction to God or replace it with a prayer. Give thanks and praise to God or meditate on Scripture. It may help you to gently repeat a phrase from the Bible, possibly breathing the words in and out as a Breath Prayer.

7 OPEN UP
Talk to God about your spiritual journey and your experience in the CHRIST stages of faith. Ask the Lord to guide you as you reflect. How do you feel about the progression of your faith? How do you feel about where you are today? What have you learned? You may want to journal your prayers and what God seems to be saying to you.

STAGES IN JESUS' LIFE

STAGE OF FAITH	JESUS' DEVELOPMENT (LUKE)
Confidence in God	Trusting God's love, including through his mother and other people (2:19, 40)
Help in Discipleship	Practice disiplines to worship God in synogogue and temple (in community), read and meditate on Scripture, fast and pray in solitude (2:41-50; 4:1)
Responsibilities in Ministry	Serving God and people as a carpenter a (4:22) and in ministries of deliverance, healing, teaching, and discipleship (4:31ff)
The Wall (Transition)	Waiting many years to launch his public ministry (3:23), being rejected by his hometown and family (4:28-29; 8:19-21), and taking up his cross (22:42 - 23:46)
Inner Journey	Baptism (3:21-22), 40-days in the wilderness (4:2-13), solitude with his Abba (5:16), and travailing in prayer in the garden (22:39-44)
Spirit-Led Ministry	Following the Spirit's leading (4:1; 5:42-44; 6:12-13), teaching with confident authority (4:32), serving God with great joy (10:21), and relying on God for miracles (e.g., 8:22-25, 42-48; 11:20)
Transforming Union	Glowing with God's presence and glory (9:28-36), abandoning his life fully to God's purpose (22:42; 23:46), and loving his enemies (e.g., 23:34, 43)

STAGES IN PSALM 23

STAGE OF FAITH	PSALM 23 (NKJV)
Confidence in Christ	"The LORD is my shepherd, I shall not want" (v. 1).
Help in Discipleship	"He makes me to lie down in green pastures; he leads me beside the still waters. He restores my soul" (vv. 2-3).
Responsibilities in Ministry	"He leads me in the paths of righteousness for his name's sake" (v. 3).
The Wall (Transition)	"Yea, though I walk through the valley of the shadow of death..." (v. 4).
Inner Journey	"I will fear no evil for you are with me; your rod and your staff they comfort me. You prepare a table before me in the presence of my enemies" (vv. 4-5).
Spirit-Led Ministry	"You annoint my head with oil; my cup runs over" (v. 5).
Transforming Union	"Surely goodness and mercy shall follow me all the days of my life; and I will dwell in the house of the LORD forever" (v. 6).

STAGES & DISCIPLINES

STAGE OF FAITH	SPIRITUAL DISCIPLINES
Confidence in Christ	Noticing God in nature, learning from spiritual leaders, reading Bible stories, attending church, praying about personal needs
Help in Discipleship	Being discipled to Jesus by a pastor/teacher, getting involved in church, daily devotions, praying the Lord's Prayer, and memorizing Bible verses
Responsibilities in Ministry	Service projects, expressing spiritual gifts, books and classes on serving/leading, discovering identity in Christ, sharing the gospel
The Wall (Transition)	Receiving spiritual care or counseling, setting boundaries, enjoying God's blessings, taking a nap, praying Psalms of lament
Inner Journey	Praying the Psalms, soul friendships (with empathy), Lectio Divina, quiet prayer, reading devotional classics, healing prayer
Spirit-Led Ministry	Watching and praying to act with Holy Spirit, abandoning outcomes to God, listening to God, abiding in prayer for self and others, secrecy (doing good deeds without recognition)
Transforming Union	Turning activity into prayer, contemplative prayer, appreciating the Trinity, staying engaged in church and community, blessing those who mistreat you

STAGES & SILENT PRAYER

STAGE OF FAITH	EXPERIENCE IN SILENT PRAYER
First Half	Often feels like desolation
Confidence in Christ	Antsy-ness, shame, doubt, or fear; feels ineffective
Help in Discipleship	Wandering thoughts and distractions may take over
Responsibilities in Ministry	Feels unproductive but may be helpful training
The Wall (Transition)	Brings up questions and emotions; may inspire longing for God
Second Half	Often feels like consolation
Inner Journey	Cultivates sense of God's presence and comfort
Spirit-Led Ministry	Facilitates hearing God's voice and following God's wisdom
Transforming Union	Fosters contemplation (simply being in God's presence) and turning work into prayer

ALSO BY BILL & KRISTI GAULTIERE

Books

Journey of the Soul

Your Best Life in Jesus' Easy Yoke

Healing Prayer

Unforsaken

Lectio Divina Guides

Ignatian Meditation Guides

Breath Prayer Guides

Sabbatical Guide

Jesus' Greatest Teaching

Emotional Intelligence

Soul Talk Cards

Journey of the Soul: Soul Talk Cards

Surprising Joy (Advent)

Visual Devotions (Journey, Rescue, & Rhythms)

**For more information
or to purchase a Soul Shepherding resource,
visit soulshepherding.org**

REVITALIZE YOUR MINISTRY AT THE SOUL SHEPHERDING INSTITUTE

Bill and Kristi Gaultiere know how hard it is to care for your own soul when you're in ministry or leading other people. That's why they developed the Soul Shepherding Institute. When your soul is being nourished in Jesus, you enjoy your work and relationships, your message compels people to Jesus, your team is activated to serve God with you, and your ministry blesses more and more people.

The Soul Shepherding Institute features a unique model of training leaders and churches to flourish spiritually and psychologically in their apprenticeship to Jesus and ministry to others. The 18-month program features four immersive, 5-day retreats with Bill and Kristi. Also you have the option to earn a certificate in the ministry of Spiritual Direction through participating in monthly online groups.

EACH RETREAT FEATURES:

- Dynamic teaching on soul care
- Individual and group spiritual direction
- Rest, solitude, and silence in beautiful surroundings
- Guided experiences for spiritual formation
- Customized spiritual and psychological coaching

You'll leave each retreat feeling rested, rejuvenated, encouraged, and equipped with the tools you need to thrive in your life, relationships, ministry, work, and leadership.

Join an exclusive community of 25 pastors and ministry leaders at one of our upcoming retreats!

LEARN MORE AND APPLY TODAY AT SOULSHEPHERDING.ORG

WEEKLY ENCOURAGEMENT IN YOUR JOURNEY WITH JESUS

In their Soul Shepherding blog and Soul Talks podcast Bill & Kristi Gaultiere invite you into authentic conversations that cultivate emotional and relational health, intimacy with Jesus, and effective leadership.

To learn more or subscribe visit soulshepherding.org

Made in the USA
Columbia, SC
16 May 2021